There is Life in This Water

The Poetry of Tishun Nikco

DearHearts Publishing

ISBN: 978-1-7361992-5-1

Cover design by: Tishun Nikco

Printed in the United States of America by DearHearts Publishing

I dedicate this book to my tribe of dear hearts who cover me in love every day; and especially younger me who fought so hard for this day. I love you all with every fiber of my being now and forever.

I dedicate this book to all the lovers out there. To all the big hearted intuitive feelers who refuse to harden their hearts in a jaded world. For anyone who has ever loved someone, for anyone who has ever lost someone, and for anyone who has had to go on with a love unrequited. Love is as essential to life as water. Love is as transformative as water and takes many forms. May we all learn to love ourselves fully and create lives we enjoy living in. For when we heal and become whole, we see that love is all around us and never left us at all. Only then do we feel the following words:

Our love has flown around the earth and now it has finally washed back ashore, home.

FOREWARD

The cover art and the following poems and artwork flowed out of me in a very short span of time similar to the prophetic scribes of long ago. My work flowed from the overflow of my heart. I wrote this book three years after falling in love with myself. *There is Life in This Water* has themes of a woman who fought to discover her voice in a desolate place. I had to reclaim my power as a spirit wrapped in flesh, a creator, and a black woman who refuses to stand at the back of the line. Adversity has built my character. I realized I have a right to be here and my words are powerful. I know my roots. I cherish my story. This book is a part of my spirit that I am now ready to share. Come on and flow with me. Let these words take you on a journey where you see yourself in this water. Come and get what you need. Take a sip, dive in, pour it on yourself, wade in it, sprinkle it, splash around, or baptize yourself in these divine waters and emerge refreshed, rejuvenated, and renewed. You are Sovereign. You are more powerful than you know. Selah.

Tishun Nikco

CONTENTS

INTRODUCTION

Special Introduction By B. Randall

Have you ever thought of the many life cycles and iterations in a droplet of water? No matter what phase you are currently in, *There is Life in this Water* reminds us of how we are uniquely purposed. Water is both ancient and new. Water refreshes us, renews us, and reminds us to thrive. Tishun Nikco uses language that flows and allows you to feel your way through. For all of us who survived the boat ride where our legacy could have died, we can see our powerful journey through the prism of each droplet soaked in this book. *There is Life in This Water* floods your soul, feels you and fills you at the same time. There is healing in every brushstroke and word penned. As a creative, Nikco speaks the language of the artist across many genres. In this collection, she urges you to release your old self for your rebirth. You will be engulfed in the art pieces chosen for this experience. The selected works of art for her debut poetry collection are calm yet bold and leave you thirsty for more. Her poetry style is fluid and her words just make sense to your soul. *There is Life in This Water* is faith, hope, joy, and truth; it burns, it soothes, and it powerfully cleanses. Tishun Nikco's words wash away what you no longer need and all that remains is you in your purest form. Enjoy the transformative experience of the dynamic collection of poems in *There is Life in This Water.*

PREFACE

Water because our gifts must always flow
  DIVINE creativity always flows

We ride on the current of faith. We travel at the speed of my faith; there is life in this water.

We flow, still flow, will flow, flow on all dear hearts, remove all barriers. Flow over, under, around, and through all.

Fluidic, cleansing, purifying, sparkling, reflective, ever -moving, energizing, prismatic, luxurious, terrifying, calming, still, quiet, rambunctious, peaceful, energetic, renewing, conductive

WATER

LOVE

GOD

Key:

There is Life in This WATER Key for Enjoying:

Poems do not start with the title.
We recognize a new poem as we recognize a raindrop-already in
motion.
Signifies the end of the poem

Chapter One: The Fount

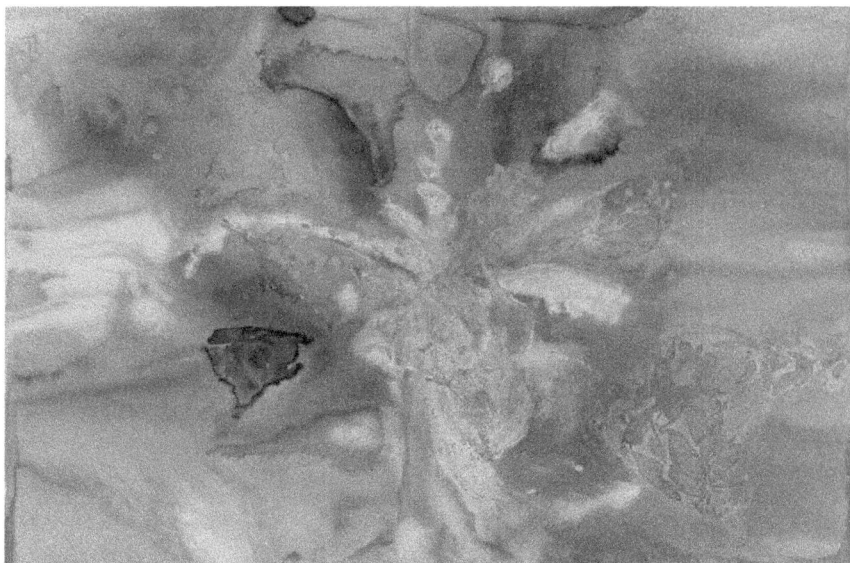

Chapter One: The Fount

We travel the speed of faith

Actually it's the speed of our faith

Not others

The unfaithful will never understand this

It's not about religion

Or ritual, shouting, or speaking in tongues

It's not about who gave me a prophetic

Word

And whether I received it or not

Chapter One: The Fount

Soul-Love & Soul Living Sunday

Motivational Monday

Thoughtful Tuesday

Wakeup! Wednesday

Thank you Thursday

Fan the flames Friday--of Friendship, fortitude

Sentimental Saturday -- Sharing, Sacred

Chapter One: The Fount

It's like water

    It's like rain

It's like truth

    It's like pain

Can we start over

      Over again

    -to everyone on religion, racism, sexism,

    boundaries drawn for countries, wars,

    consumerism, poverty.....using people and

    loving things...

Chapter One: The Fount

Sober Poet

Paint is my drug of choice

And words my symphony

Blissfully content with

A dictionary

A Thesaurus

And my dreams

A pad, a pen

Some clay

Some pigments

Torn paper

I paint with words

I sculpt novels

I write visions, compositions

I see worlds that don't quite yet exist

I paint the love I have

And the love I always wanted

I paint the world

I always wanted to live in

Breathe in

Swim in

Love in and out of

Fully

Completely

Chapter One: The Fount

You call it art

They are all maps of my life

Keys to my journey

Treasure maps to my heart

Places visited

Destinations I still crave

Stories in images

My life

And lives unlived

Legacies revealed

The essence of secrets

Desire vs. Value

Knowledge vs. Application

Hell vs. Heaven

Acceptance vs. Exemption

Drought vs. Love

Restoration vs. Stabilization

Story vs. glory

Darkness vs. Light

Reality vs. possibility

Singleness vs. solitude

Battles, warrings that go on and on

Chapter One: The Fount

Themes of my life

If and when they ask me which

Writers are my greatest inspiration

I'll start with my father

My mother

My grandmothers

My grandfathers

My sisters

Then Harriet Tubman,

Sojourner Truth, and Maya Angelou

And many, many more

Some are no longer seen

They tell me they are not all writers

However, I say they are indeed

Because the greatest stories

May not be printed on bound pages

Your life is the most profound story you will ever tell

I have read some of the most prolific stories

By observing and witnessing lives

Actions taken

Lovers gained,

Love lost

Chapter One: The Fount

Dreams deferred, killed, snuffed out

Talent developed

Talents misused, abused, extorted, aborted

Freedom fought for

Lives redeemed

Innovations, ideas siphoned off

Creative genius celebrated

Creative genius overlooked

And all these stories have become a part of me

We are the living sequels passed down

From writers who wrote inwardly instead of externally

Who begat us in love, living prose and poetry

The most talented are in the graveyard

And were never recognized for their genius

I write with them too

       -They write with me

Chapter One: The Fount

Every man

I meet came from a woman

Why don't we love our women

Protect our women

Fight for our woman

Provide for our women

You are more than half a woman

Loving her

Is loving yourself

Love a Woman

Drink her tears

Pray her strength

Love her insecurities

Love her fears

Love her imperfections

Love her past

Her present

Her future

Love her journey

Her burdens

Her healing

The full power of her love

Chapter One: The Fount

Hold her body

And cherish her heart

Loving her and embracing her pain

Releases all the love

For you

She's been holding back

Let the rivers

Of love flow

      -Selah

Chapter Two: These Transformative Waters

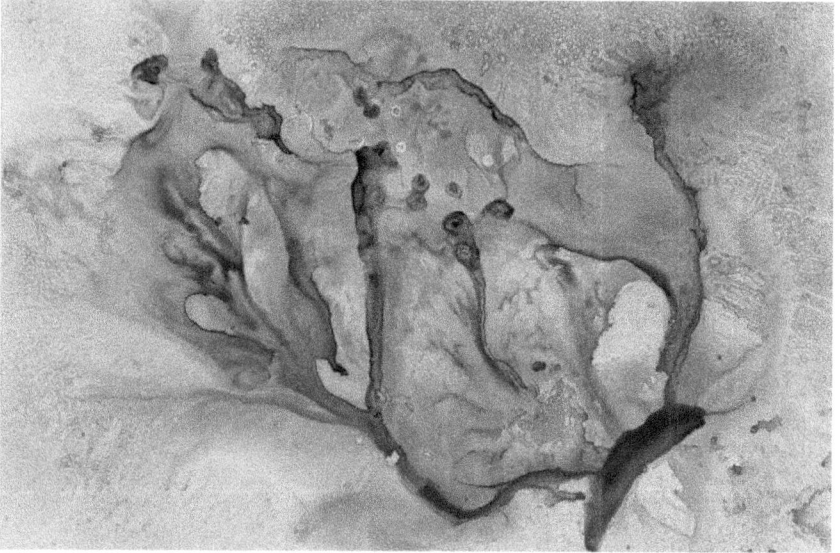

We are ARTISTS, CREATORS

We are seeds and soil

Farmers and Fisherwomen,

Butterflies, Swans, Salt, Light, & Love

TRAVELERS from a foreign land,

More than world citizens

We may never know our home galaxy

We ARE Bridges, Transformers, and Conductors

Innovators, Engineers, & Inventors

We turn pain to power

We turn fear to fuel

We propel energy forward

We bridge where you are to

Where you always wanted to be

We are mirrors and visionaries

We turn Heartbreaks into Breathtaking ART

We are the flower that was once was a

Single seed

Who had to break through

The earth

Towards an unseen sky

After digging deep

Chapter Two: These Transformative Waters

buried in the dirt, forgotten, isolated

lonely

We artists had to grow inward

Long before we were strong enough to break the shell

In the darkest of night

Who knew those deep roots

Would make us so strong?

Artists bloomed one petal

At a time

Our colors, our fragrance, our aura now

draws your attention

your adoration, your time

Artists are warriors who had to know

Recognize, believe, and fight for their own

Value and worth, while hidden from view

Still buried

Still underground

Still unaware themselves

Of how or when they would bloom

Artist are Lovers and Storytellers

Chapter Two: These Transformative Waters

With knocked knees and chattering teeth

We keep telling our stories

IN ALL MEDIUMS.

1 day =

1440 minutes

1 day =

86400 seconds

480 minutes I sleep I rest (8 hours)

28,800 seconds (8 hours)

1440-480= 960 minutes I spin sunlight

86400-28800= 57,600 seconds of daylight

Burning daylight

I fish

I farm

Chapter Two: These Transformative Waters

Lonely Lovers

Cloaked in colorful coats

Vibrant pigment-soaked rich tapestry

Some of the most elaborate

Stained glass windows to such tender souls

They see so much

Lonely lovers are so sensitive

And yet they must experience this

World as visitors

Keep these ethereal hearts

Emitting iridescent hues

Lonely lovers are dazzling and divine

Their solitude perplexing to the naked eye

Their magnificence should be shared

However the lonely lover

Has a history of desire competing with value

Care versus attraction

A lonely lover would rather be an admired,

wild, growing, free flower

Than a plucked imprisoned one

Kept in a lovely vase

we live on a solitary plane

Chapter Two: These Transformative Waters

We dance between the raindrops

We tiptoe on each grain of sand

We surf on emotions

We are living legends who

May be celebrated now or

After we are gone

Petals blown in the wind like the

Dandelions or the memory of honeysuckle tea

Chapter Two: These Transformative Waters

Insane lover

Love is insane

Doing the same thing over and over again

Expecting different results

You have to be proficiently crazy to love

No loan officer would ever give

Out a loan to build love

It's not a good investment

Who knows if you will ever get a return on

Love

Love keeps coming back

Keeps jumping back on the horse

After falling off a million times

Love keeps hoping

Beyond sameness

Believing beyond

Doubt

Trusting beyond betrayal

That we can be better

That we can do better

That we are better than we have

Ever shown

That we can give what we never did receive

And appreciate what we never had

Love keeps going

On nothing

A car running with no fuel

A broken light bulb somehow shining

Yet there's a power shortage

An unplugged radio still playing

With no battery

Love is a miracle

One that we all need

Crave

Desire

It will never make sense

Love is not a logical toy

She is the essence of all

She is the forest and the trees

Love is in every tree

And every breath we take

Every child conceived

Love is the cosmos in a single cell

Love is the ocean in a drop

Chapter Two: These Transformative Waters

Love travels in the speed of our awareness

The speed of our faith

A well that will never dry

We see love as far away

But love is here to stay

The blind can see her

The deaf can hear her

Taste, touch, see, and hear

Love is no longer a stranger

Be a fool and dance with love

She's insane and we'd

Be happier if we went insane

And loved just for love's sake

And then we may realize we've been the crazy

One all along

Trying to live without her

I have loved and nurtured

The little girl

Inside me

I love her

I have loved her

And forever will

She has been through so much

I comfort her

And wipe her infinite tears away

Into a spiritual bucket

Every night I gingerly

pour her tears into a well

I carry her with me

I bathe in oceans of soul love

Less salty, more sweet

Self-replenishing, always renewing

Purifying

She sojourns to the rivulets with me,

Discovering hidden waterfalls

One day her well filled so

That we allowed you to bring your cup

To drink in the overflow

Chapter Two: These Transformative Waters

To bask in the overglow

Together we sat on the edge of her well

To share soul to soul

One day you convinced me to jump in

To go into myself, share my pain

And

    I

        Jumped

I splashed into myself

And we both saw more than intimacy

My well expanded for two

As we swam, swirled, and soaked

It all in

My well became an ocean,

With just us

And we realized we

Had become love

We had leaped in love together

We were completely enveloped

In every single direction

Love was all around us

Yet more than a body

was removed

When you left

The home for our love

was demolished

I lost the

Whole ocean

The overflow gone

The well drained

Replaced with despair

LOVE left

After you smashed our hopes

To pieces smaller than the

Grains of sand

Now under our feet

Our ocean became my desert

when you left

I named it after your desertion

And I began my tireless work

of carrying her tears

Once again

Enraged I watched

the buckets fill faster than ever

Chapter Two: These Transformative Waters

So now, I must carry

My little girl back to her ocean

For she has already forgotten the way

And I fret she will forget how to

    Swim

        Again

           -Never forget

Chapter Two: These Transformative Waters

I love you

Your heart has been broken a

Million times and you still

Love again

You glow

Your words form a melody

A monologue

My favorite mantra

Beauty in not just the words

You say but also the way

You say them

The way they fall like petals

From your lips

or emerge free

And fly from your heart to mine

How can I love you more

I love your little girl

Your grown woman

Your elder

Your saint

Your sinner

Your lover, your inventor, your seductress

Chapter Two: These Transformative Waters

Your visionary, your fool, your creature, your remixer

Your everywoman, your leader, your servant

Your nurturer

I'm home with you

I take you with me, in me

Everywhere I go

How can I LOVE you more

I must protect you from the winds of

Doubt

The darts of

Jealousy

The cruelty of envy

The perils of not understanding

Your valleys

The isolation of GENIUS

The pain of loneliness

The lashes of betrayal

I must teach you to

Stay congruent with yourself

To always reach for yourself

To revolve on your own axis

Stay bold, brave, decisive, fearless

Chapter Two: These Transformative Waters

You do not need their approval

Or their validation

You traded empty likes

And you FEAST on Divine Love

-you, me, us

Chapter Three: Turbulence (I Ain't Here For You)

Chapter Three: Turbulence (I Ain't Here For You)

I traded likes

For soul love

I left them

At the crossroads a long time ago

I am present for love

Open for the moments

I don't live for the posts

I don't search for the spotlight

I gaze into your face

I feast in all that you are

Each expression noteworthy

You are a masterpiece I would hate

To miss

How can I share

What is not mine

I'm visiting this moment in time

I do not own it

I need not attempt

To repackage it for the masses

Our love is not commercial

Let me only bask in this moment

Tenderly record every detail into

Chapter Three: Turbulence (I Ain't Here For You)

My mind

Commit it to my long-term memory

Remember us tonight

How you look

How we feel

Savoring every

Flavor, nuance

Spice, herb, sprinkle

Tint, shade, angle

Calculation, addition, subtraction

My latitude and your longitude

The elevation of your smile

This space, our time, the pattern

The light makes as it dances

Across your face

All that's relative at this point-

Where our lives intersect

To create this perspective

For me to walk through

The gallery of our love

And our art is not for sale

Chapter Three: Turbulence (I Ain't Here For You)

I am not here for public consumption

I'm not for sale

I'm no longer part of this zoo

I'm not prostituting my gifts

I'm not begging for your approval

Validation

Or blessing

I know you did not create me and neither will you control

me

I'm no longer listening to your empty words

Waiting on your empty promises

I'm no longer feeding myself on your lies

I no longer believe in your love void of action, void of

affection

I do not believe you can enforce God's law

Without upholding

       Her love

Chapter Three: Turbulence (I Ain't Here For You)

Please Don't Fuck With me

I'm a lion behind this curtsy

There's a scream behind my smile

I am a peaceful warrior

I love

I enjoy life

However

The lover never forgot her fight

Because all too often

People want to shit on the calm

Want to wreck paradise

Shatter an oasis

With their chaos

And you have to come out of

A good book or

child's pose

or a bird of paradise

To check a bitch

I don't stay there

I love my happy place

I live here

And I'll swiftly shut you down

Chapter Three: Turbulence (I Ain't Here For You)

If you attempt to bulldoze it

I am my home

I must belong to me

Before I share myself with another

Just stay in your lane

I do no harm

But I take no mess

Yes I watch

I pray

And I fight

Gentle like a dove

But like a snake

I know when to bite

I already read your tea leaves

Now please don't fuck with me

Chapter Three: Turbulence (I Ain't Here For You)

Today my hand graced a pecan tree

very dear to me

planted by my grandfather

upon my entry

into this world

a single seed

my seed planted in fertile Houstonian soil

all my roots began from this very spot

as I touch the leaves I think of all this tree gives

That started with a single seed

A seed that was unseen

Yet growing all the way

To break ground is

A birthday

The darker the times,

The deeper the roots.

The deeper the roots,

The stronger the tree.

I am reminded of what this means to me

These roots have been my strength

Propelling me to move towards the light

I stand tall and absorb the sun

my leaves dance to the rhythm of the wind

As I live in the light

I produce life-giving food

I am thankful for those dark times where I felt hidden

A treasure in disguise

My shell cracked and transformed

I grew wise

I became more than a solitary seed

I became a survivor

I am thankful for the heavy rains that hit my face but

provided what I needed for the droughts

I am thankful for the bark that protects my heart

Many leaves keep me sensitive to all life around me.

I can produce healing strength,

nourishment for weary souls,

shade for scorching times

I've gone from survivor to provider

My fruit is new life

Chapter Four: These Converging Waters

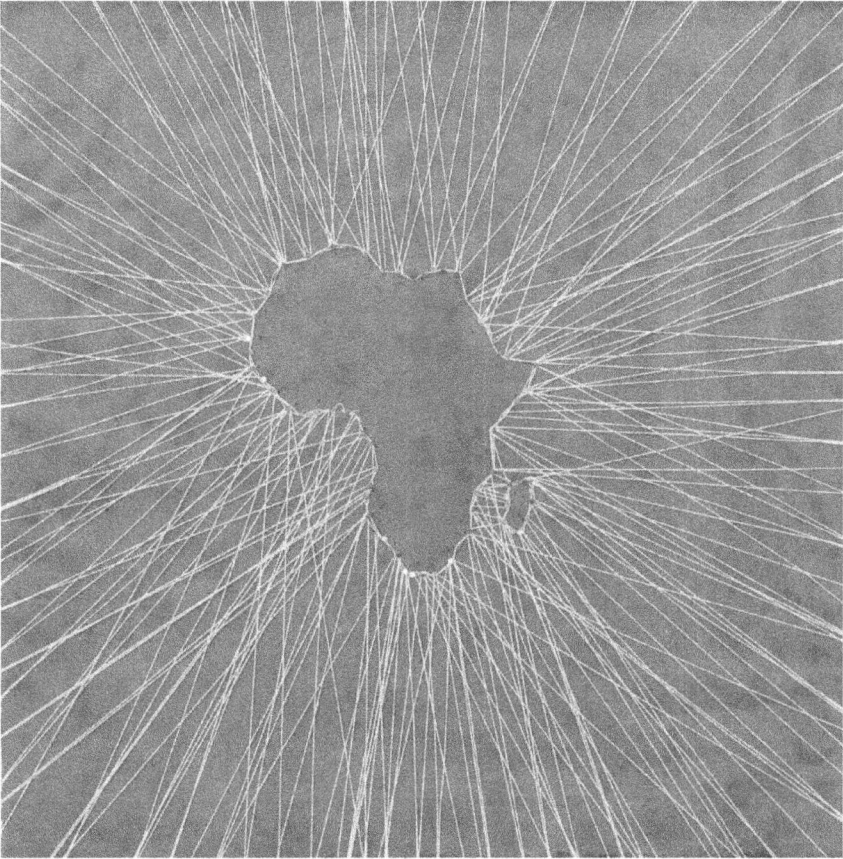

Chapter Four: These Converging Waters

We were created from the DIVINE

the immortal, self-renewing, all in-compassing

We are the leaves, seeds, and flowers

eternity holds us at the tips

flows through us

gives us all we have

all we will ever need

at the proper time we must go

to grow

Wind can push us to our destiny

and we were created to go deep

to steady ourselves

to transform ourselves

after choosing our own sacred place

to grow

if we stay shallow

be become only brittle dust

when the final winds blow

Chapter Four: These Converging Waters

A long time ago

I finally grew up

When I made peace with it all

When I forgave it all

And started living

For me

My mom felt that

And I saw she was proud

She is my home

Country

My first lessons

Learned Inside her gates

I honor her

Infinite rings of beauty

Elegance and grace

Her glowing skin

My Warrior Queen

I am fruit

From her tree planted

by still waters

I am a part of the whole

And her tears are in my smile

Chapter Four: These Converging Waters

Her grievances in my laughter

Her voice in my song

She held the Map

Of infinity in each leaf

A symphony of secrets

Chime every time the wind blows

In every ring a novel

Her bark, her sap

Her roots, her glory, her story

All evident inside

Of me

     -My Queen Warrior Mother

Chapter Four: These Converging Waters

The black woman loves the deepest

The widest

The most potent, rich, long lasting

The most powerful

Tell me what love could stretch thousands

Of years and kiss me today

Love evident in the arch of my back

Love in the upward curls of praise

That adorn my crown

The blanket of melanin that hugs

My body as a silk scarf

A world I see from diamond and onyx eyes

The black woman's love has been weighed

Measured, and tested

She bore children she would never hold

Never see her grow old

Or acknowledge that she is their mother

She nurtured souls

Classified as imports

Goods, cattle

She became a linguist

The black woman transformed

Translated her rich heritage, folded up her sovereignty

Her intellect

Her royalty

Her wisdom

Her creativity

And whispered it into her babies' ears

She folded herself into herself

To enter your narrow door

She had to gift wrap beautiful parts of herself

She buried them at your gate

She kept record even if only in her heart

She loved stronger than strong

With all she had left

A remnant of her full glory

Her roar became a song

Her song became a whisper

Whose wind

Was felt under her feet

She flew

Barely above the ground

A silent soar you cannot see or hear

The black woman kept alive

Chapter Four: These Converging Waters

A love that wanted to soar to the heavens

Chained with a reality that slung

Her back to hell

Time and time again

The black woman has loved in Hell

Longed for earth

And dreamed of heaven

Longed for a dirt bed instead of coals

The black woman's love is the strongest

Because she had to push through

A hell she neither created

Nor deserved

Her strength grew

She is the most beautiful warrior

The Black Woman

Our Queen Mother Warriors

Taught us to hope despite the odds

Our Queen Mother Warriors

Begat Hope, Begat Love

I am love repackaged and remixed

Chapter Four: These Converging Waters

From some of the greatest leaders

To ever draw breath.

-One Queen Mother Warrior to Another

Chapter Four: These Converging Waters

I am here

Been here

Eyes opened wide

I am the talent you go out and seek

What you search for

I already have

But you'd rather reject me

Instead of connecting me to what is

Rightfully mine

linking me to my purpose

I am intimate with your rejection

yet I know it is not divine rejection

she brought me here at the right,

appointed time

And I'm not turning back to

The all too familiar feeling

Of seeing an opportunity

With my name on it

Handed right to someone else

Because of so many prejudices

That have nothing to do with me

You push me aside

And run to someone

who secretly hates you

yet smiles in your face

With not even an inkling of

all that I had for you

You fight me to go grasp

dwindling embers

worse than hunger you don't even realize your starvation

as you consume decay instead

of life

I am finally at peace with it all

since I packed and left

    -Intimate with Rejection

Black Butterfly

Education is power

All these titles

Am I worthy now?

I am the most educated

Demographic in America

Run the Usher Board?

Run all the church ministries?

I'll do it

I'll do it

I don't get tired

I pay my tithes & my offerings

I do it

I pay them double by faith

while I'm hungry

I raise the children with or without you

I'll do it

they are your gifts to me

Straighten my hair? I'll do it

Am I pretty yet?

Beat myself up for being single?

I'll do it

Buy all your books?

That tell me to work on myself

And hopefully one day

I can be chosen to be a wife

I bought them

Read them all twice

Hold you down for whatever you do?

Hold down the family?

Hold down the church?

Hold down the community?

I'll do it

I've done it

Work and support your dreams?

I'll do it

Workout, lose some weight, build some ass?

Buy it, or steal it

I'll get that ass because you like it

Gotta have something

a man can hold on to

I'll do it

Cook your meals?

I become a chef

Chapter Four: These Converging Waters

Wash your clothes?

You'll never touch dirty clothes again

Be sexy?

I buy out the lingerie store

Take all the pole dancing classes

Become a bedroom gymnast

I do that, and that, and that

You are my King

And when I turn on the television

I see you with a woman

Who paid for synthetic melanin

Paid for lip injections,

Paid for butt implants

has no thighs

and doesn't pray

she doesn't cook, or clean

I see a woman who helps you

build nothing

Holds no degrees

And bought more hair

To extend her naturally limp tendrils

A woman you wait on

Chapter Four: These Converging Waters

Hand and foot

You marry her quick

And have a ton of children

You cook and clean for them all

I'm single and I listen

I hear you praise her

for nothing more than existing while

I fight the world every day to love you

But I will not fight you to love you

Everyone asks me

Are you mad?

I hold my head up high

Of course not

And go home and cry

Who is going to fight for me?

       - Black Butterfly I

Chapter Four: These Converging Waters

The light hurts my eyes

It's uncomfortable

Unnerving

Delivered from emotional cataracts

Perception on how we see

I open my eyes

I see scars from my pain

But I also see colors I've only imagined

I see the music

Notes that encouraged

Me

Gave me hope

I walk on vibrations

I see the rough edges and smooth planes

I feel with my eyes now

I'm overwhelmed by the beauty

The light hurts my eyes

I see beauty in the imperfections

The cracks

The scars form lovely patterns

Chapter Four: These Converging Waters

Brilliant Black Butterfly

Do you even know how beautiful you are?

The rich melody in each

Flap of your wings

The mosaic of colors

Patterns

Telling your story

mapping how far you've come

You fly with wings

You never knew you had

Transformed from darkness

You never knew would end

What was pain is now power

The most beautiful story

You're a survivor

Black onyx in the sky

They chase you

But will never catch up

Your dream broke free

When you emerged

Your flight is

faith metamorphosized

Chapter Four: These Converging Waters

Out of your darkness

New wings emerged

And you traded your life for

endless skies

You could barely move

But now you fly

You crawled

And now you Fly

You cried

In your isolated tomb

You thought you'd die

But now you fly

You trace the sun in

The most purposeful

The most determined

The most breathtaking Flight

   -Fly Brilliant Black Butterfly, Fly

Chapter Five: The Evaporation

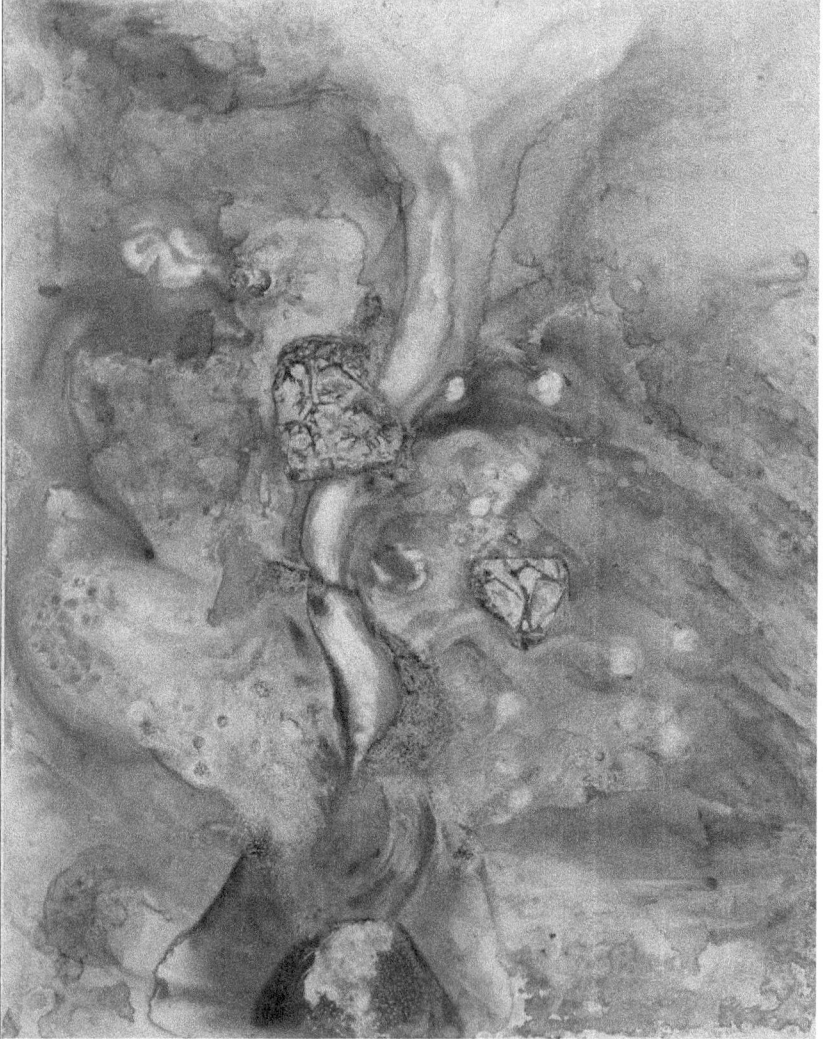

Chapter Five: The Evaporation

Betraying yourself is the worst

When you siphon off yourself

For someone else's thirst

Selling parts of yourself that you need

For someone else's greed

Silencing your voice

For someone else's dream

J.O.B.

Just Over Broke

Paycheck to paycheck living

Is this a joke?

They say

be thankful you have a job

While they pray for payday

Wishing their lives away

After five minutes into Monday,

Asking me where is Friday?

You know where it is

You're older than me

You are a cautionary tale

There is no vacation or cruise

you can make to take away the

Every day misery

I saw zombies walking around

Everyday

Is this what we are here for?

A J.O.B. that turns a beautiful life

into a bore

Work done by 10, but I'm held captive

until 4

Waving fake goodbyes

a few hours till shut eye

my freedom flies by

Alarm rings at 6 am

And it's time to go back

For more?

Am I the new slave?

Selling hours of my life

for an insufficient price

How much will you pay for

My time?

What is the worth of a life?

20, 30, 50 thou?

- J.O.B. I

2, 4, 6, 8

Hard to eat with so few dollars on my plate

The bank statement never

Reveals my true worth

Living off cents when my creativity is infinite

I chase my dreams

While my bills chase me

Time is money?

that will never be

What a self-unfulfilling prophecy

Chapter Five: The Evaporation

The same routine day in

Day out

No credit for the workers

Praise reserved for the ones with clout

The insecure, and jealous lead

Glorified supervisors who don't own a thing

Fueled by prejudice, power, and greed

Coveting and hiding those with the innate ability

To lead

I may get a promotion if my boss leaves

wait for it

In 30 years I might get social security

A half hearted thank you and a watch

I can try to retire

but plan B is a Walmart greeter

too busy to play with my grandkids

And use my gifted watch to track

my golden years ticking away

No, I'll be crazy and live off the endless creativity

Ingenuity granted to me

I'll stay obedient to divine directives

No man or woman provides my daily bread

I've turned the chapter from desperation

to joyful expectation

My faith is not in your check

I choose me; checkmate

The divine has imparted wisdom in my spirit

I walk a path lovingly created for only me

I am clothed in the royal garments of eternity

As I skip off into my destiny

-J.O.B. no more

Chapter Five: The Evaporation

The hope of time travel is a luxury

One I cannot afford

My past is gone

She has no latitude, longitude

She has no address

Sight, smell, touch, or taste

She only resides deep inside me

Frequenting exclusive circles

In my mind

She dances well into the night

Keeping me awake

Playing the reel of my life

And then she retreats

Back

And I remember my past is lost

Gone never to materialize on this plane

Again

I take pictures every time I blink

To capture the moments that develop

Into memories

Where I examine the meaning later

Again and again

Snapshots of a world I can no longer

Breathe in

A forever fleeting past

Created even as we speak

These moments have formed a dynamic life

One I would happily live again

To enjoy the moments I did not

Fully actualize

      -TIME

Chapter Five: The Evaporation

The Past is Gone

All we have is the memory

We can keep the good

And leave the bad

Easier said than done

Often because the bad and ugly

Are on the reverse side

Of the same coin

The pain right after the joy

Hell after heaven

Flowers blown from my hands

A balloon sailing the winds

Up and away out of my sight

Scalding tears erupt from

A boiling heart

They escape down my face

steam off a cool cheek

as they travel a long way from home

Each one a melted dream

An ocean in a drop

A novel unread

A deconstructed hope

Chapter Five: The Evaporation

Deferred

Transfigured moments I can no

Longer relive

A love I can no longer reach

Untouchable

And fading fast from view

Never again to bask in the radiance

Joy now clouded in grief

I am left

Cold abandoned

Alone

A Lone soul

A Lone life

Let my heart soak in this moment

The one before I started this poem

Already over?

That moment is gone

And this one

and that one

forever gone

For this poem was a tunnel

And I emerge different than before

What will we do with

These precious stones we have left

The emeralds that fall from us

One pours from our soul every second

And the jewels create the map

Of all we touch

What pattern, what picture will you create?

What designs do you have left to draw?

With your footsteps?

                    - TIME II

Chapter Five: The Evaporation

I am a stranger

In this house

I built

A house that has never been my home

Though you have slumbered

Feasted, danced, sang here, loved here

Raised families here, married here

Inherited wealth here

I have not

I have not rested in this house

I could never call it home

The nightmares still haunt me in the day

By sunset I am too exhausted to sleep

I weep, a Trail of Tears Middle Passage Sized, I weep

Anyone would think it is mine

For the time I have invested in it

Laying down each brick

The cornerstones carved from my bones

The length, the width, the depth

Comprised of melanin, spirituals, prayers

The beat of distant drums, seas of cotton, evaporated

mother's milk,

my mother's very breath

I built this house while being choked of my hope

Raped of my dreams

Beaten into submission

My children stolen, abused

Turned into the very brick and mortar used

to place the foundation where I grit and bore

The lashes

I built this house, America, all the while

-Homeless

Chapter Five: The Evaporation

I preach with a different medium

You take the pulpit

I'll take the pasture

I traded bondage

For freedom a long time ago

See, I arrived tattered

Bruised

Hungry, Sore

Thirsty for more

Ready for a new life

What I found was a beautiful new land

More illuminated than I could

Ever have imagined

The sunlight danced on my face

And yet my feet were the same

My path was made new

Yet as I searched for a

Cool drank

My thirst was not translatable in

A foreign land

Their faces and everything there

Questioned not only my words

Chapter Five: The Evaporation

But my whole existence

I had crossed a line

And went from

A What

To a Who

A transformation from a thing

To a human being

A human who clung to

Every shred of dignity to

Cross the invisible line

To be the free woman

I always knew I already was

However, I was greeted by no one

I was a liberated stranger in a

Foreign land

I had no lover

No mother

No brother

No father

No sister

No family to hold my hand

And enjoy my freedom with me

Chapter Five: The Evaporation

No one to share my newfound splendor

My laughter

My tears of joy

And sorrow for those

Lost to captivity

No one to wrap

Arms around me as a love letter

Personified and say

Welcome Daughter....

So I came back

But I didn't come to preach

I came to teach

I came to reach

Out my new hands

And reach out my new feet

And bring my family out

You can take the pulpit

I'll take the pasture

The rivers, the lakes

The shacks,

The outhouses

The mansions

Chapter Five: The Evaporation

The parks

I'll take all the places

Where my kin are toiling

Turning, birthing, dying,

Straining to bring out another

Man's dream instead of his own

I came back

(into your captivity)

Because I have become a free,

Human Bridge of a Woman

Here to lead my people to become

Free

Like me

I know they already are

They were created by God this way

Yet they do not live it

For they have locked freedom

away

Deep inside forgotten parts of themselves

Their innate free, powerful

Selves longs to feel the wind upon

Sun-kissed skin again to be who

Chapter Five: The Evaporation

We were going to be

Before the world told us who we were

Meant to be

I don't need your pulpit

I go where my people are

And I don't really need your doilies or your lace

no gloves

no stockings

Prayer cloths, ankle skirts

Dresses, or etiquette

is needed to save these exquisite souls

You take the pulpit

I'll take the pasture

you preach, but I teach

With my life

As I scream, "Freedom!!!"

while running with bare feet

After cutting the chains and setting

All the mental slaves free

-Ode to Harriet Tubman

Chapter Six: The Resurgence

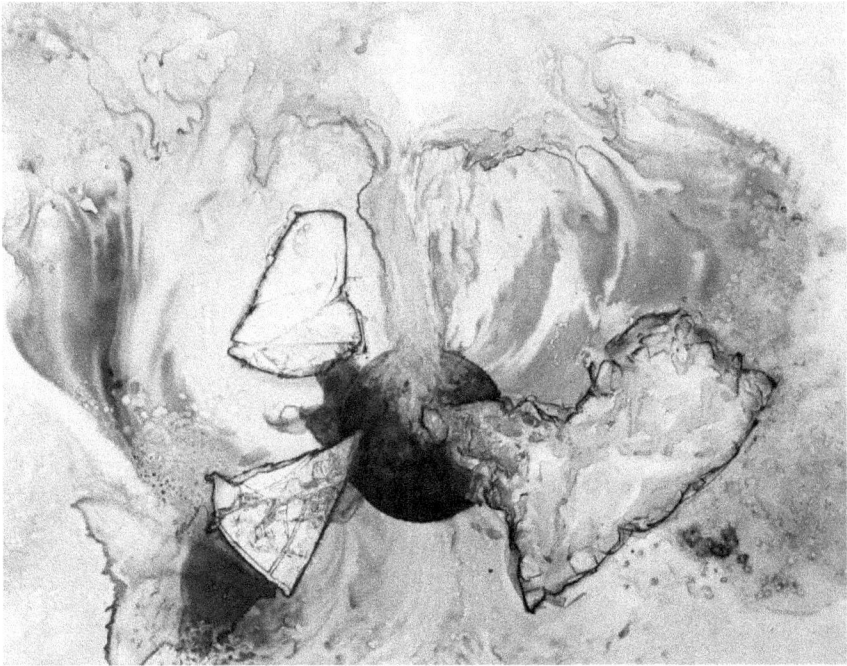

Chapter Six: The Resurgence

What makes me cry is

Everyone in their heart recognizes the beauty of sun-kissed
melanin

But the people cloaked in it, gifted by our creator with it

Everyone knows how talented, gifted, and powerful the
African diaspora is

Except for the people richer than the cosmos, forever
connected

Why else would propaganda

Disguised as high fashion

Reject chocolate hued models?

Yet promote all the fair to

Beg steal and borrow

Lips, hips, buttocks, and tans

Deep toasted cinnamon roll tans

Why would propaganda

Disguised as history books

Omit, overlook, and whitewash

So much of history?

Did the pyramids build themselves?

Explain the compound interest

Owed to me

on the profits from the sale of my

great....great...great....great....great....great....great......

.....great.....great....great...great.....great...great.....great....

great....great.....great....great.....great.....great.....great...

...great......great.....great.....great....great.....great...great

....

GREAT

Grandparents

Acknowledge how propaganda dulled your own

humanity

And why your vision is distorted to this day

Quick quiz: Who dies a black father or a puppy?

Which banks were founded on redeemed slave bonds when

slavery was abolished?

Why won't they eat the peaches in Natchez, Mississippi?

Who burned down and bombed all the Black Wall Streets?

Who put freeways and interstates through thriving black

communities?

How many black business owners were lynched?

Tell me when America was great?

And who built it?

Chapter Six: The Resurgence

Tell me how you whitewashed my religion, my culture, my heritage

Tell me how you created Christ to oppress me

Tell me the truth about Haiti

Why do Egyptologists hide my history in the Vatican?

Aren't we the prototype of civilization?

Why do you want my people ignorant and downtrodden?

How does racism really serve you?

I'll wait

[crickets..........laughter]

I laugh at you!

Did you think I was really waiting for you to answer?

I snuck in a comedy show

I have asked and answered these questions without your help

I know you will never admit the truth

I will not march or beg for you to do so either

I will not beg for your acceptance

I will not beg for your validation

I will not beg for your inclusion

THIS is why I must teach my people

THIS is why I fight to elevate our esteem

Chapter Six: The Resurgence

THIS is why I strain to raise our vibration

This is why I spread awareness and love for the forgotten

This is why I speak for the voiceless

This is why I spread love for the dynamic melanin we were born in.

-The Answer

Chapter Six: The Resurgence

Red Rivers

Red rivers still flow

They flow with the blood of our

Slaughtered sons and our slaughtered daughters

Our red rivers have furnished "your" oceans

Red from our life's source

Blood, tears, bone, marrow

Our unlived years

Our hopes, our children's fears,

Our fantasies of freedom

To one day wake up and just be

No longer having to constantly

Protect, defend, hide, prove

Our worth

Just be the people who

Mothered and fathered this earth

Our red rivers flow with

Blood we needed to be a whole people

To bond us together as husband and wife

Our hymens have washed upon

This shore

Our plasma, mother's milk,

Chapter Six: The Resurgence

Countless placentas from the unborn

Our umbilical cords tied to your greed

Who we are has always been desired and of need

For we taught the world

Yet we are now starved

malnourished on what you

Replaced our sun with

Left scared and brainwashed

We've shed more blood than the cross

More blood than all your wars

More taken souls than the stars

How do we mourn for souls we will never know?

How do we cry from beaten dried eyes?

Blood clouds our vision

We will never see all that could have been

Those lives now live only in our voice

Our legacy

Our imagination

Our melanin

Our determination

Red rivers flow through our dreams

Nourish our roots

Chapter Six: The Resurgence

Push our feet

Where we were baptized

Held down in these red rivers

Our hopes died

native tongue tied

And we came up forever changed

Disfigured, dismembered, disjointed

Can we freely give what we no longer own?

Or forfeited our right to claim?

We must redeem our lives

Dive deep to reclaim

Our stolen allegiance imbedded in

The red rivers flowing on

    The white

        And into

            the blue

    -We are the pledge

Chapter Six: The Resurgence

VOW I:

With this ring I give you my heart

I promise from this day forward

You shall not walk alone

Let my love be your refuge

Your warmth

Let my arms always be your home

I share not only my heart

and all of my affections

I share my life

everything I am

and everything I will ever be

Sunrises to sunsets

And all the nuances in between

Loving you is orbiting the sun

Every day I feel the sun

On both sides

With you.

VOW II:

I never knew loving you would change me

grow me, inspire me

I am still amazed at the joy

You bring into my life

the joy of seeing myself

Transformed by your love

A love that loves me for exactly

Who I am

Yet inspires me to reach higher

To touch my best self

In a reflection that is me

Yet more fulfilled than I ever imagined

You've shown me what love can do

I will spend the rest of my life thanking

you with my love

my devotion

my awe

VOW III:

You deserve my best

You are love personified

A true gift from God

one who unwraps me everyday

I will always do my best to give you

All that I have

Because each day you give me

The richest fullest

Most sincere love

Any man could ever want

A love I never knew I needed

A love I can not imagine my life without

And I'll never stop showing my gratitude

to God and you

For granting me a once-in-a-million

chance to hold, cherish, and LOVE my own angel

Chapter Six: The Resurgence

Dissatisfied with

Distractions and detours

Of our destiny

We both went to work

We are love

We plant love

We nourish love

We grow love

We both labor in the harvest

Of love we planted

Which has grown and brought forth

The most delicious

The most decadent fruit

We reach up to pick some

And our bare hands touched

Surprised we fell

Into the beautiful abyss

Together

What's in a man's soul?

I don't know do you?

But if he is your husband, lover, soul's mate

Then what composes his soul

is a reflection of you

If only you had the time

We could have our own civilization

A culture

A nation

A language

We could be so close that when I cut you bleed

When you hurt

    I grieve

And if I was blind

    You'd see for me

I want us to be our own society

A private club for you and me

A place we both can be free

Free from society's domination

    Free from racial, economic

        And social oppression

And the regressions of life

Chapter Six: The Resurgence

I could be ten times closer than a wife

Like a soul split in two

I'll take the left half

And leave the right half for you

I don't want to be your sun and moon

I want to be the tangible love that lies

Right next to you

Ready to comfort and hold you

Be my incarnate dream,

Let's fly to rainbow skies

I want us to soar

To glide on the smooth sides of life

And swim around or walk over the hard sides

If love is a roller coaster

You can lie on my shoulder

Together we don't say we can't

We both know we can

Does the sun rise and set from east to west?

We will let it set with your head upon my chest

And listen to my heartbeat

Ba bump, ba bump, ba bump, ba bump, ba bump

Beat to the tum tum drums of

Chapter Six: The Resurgence

Mesmerizing jazz and negro spirituals

Let our black love be more than a ritual

And when I listen to your heart

I hear almost the same beat

I must not out of excitement retreat

No, I'll stay and let our souls meet

Catch up on times missed and times gone

Catch up on lovely times present

    And lovely times to come.

To sit beside me and talk for a while

    To sneak a peak into your eyes

For you to breathe the air I breathe

And you to sneak gazes at me

For me to look into your eyes

    And for you to know that I know

You're looking deep into mine

How monumental to feel a feeling so sublime

I could just talk

    And sit with you for all time

What is in your soul?

I don't know, can you see?

But if you are to be my husband, lover, soulmate

Then what's in your soul is a reflection of me

Or what is in my soul is a reflection

and it wants to be right here next to you

So our souls can play, dance, tickle each other

And romance

    Whisper sweet nothings to each other

As we sleep in a moonlit trance

as we lay on a sea of possibilities

    Together climb mountains to our dreams

Watch sun rises

    And the volcanoes erupt

Listen to rain fall at night

    Or place freshly picked berries in our cups

As I play in your hair

    Or you play in mine

As you rub my feet

    No, I'll rub yours, now there's a good time

The faces you make

    Are quite unbelievable

the good love we could make

    Is highly achievable

You are and could be

Chapter Six: The Resurgence

The partner in my rhymes, my dreams

My hope for tomorrow all in one

I don't know what to do

The Divine finally brought me to you

And you are my muse

What's in a man's soul?

I don't know, do you?

But if he is to be your husband, lover, or soul's mate

Then what is in his soul

Must be a reflection of you

The place where I am is where

I always wanted to be

And I am not trying to conform myself

To make you my destiny

But if feels like in another life

I was your husband

and you were my wife

I want to be so close that when

I look into your eyes

I see your eyes looking into mine

And my eyes looking into the reflection

of your eyes for a second time

Chapter Six: The Resurgence

I don't want to be your everything

I just want to be your sweetest, special thang

Let my love fly from me to encircle you

And come back to me as a boomerang

From your heart, let love sing

Let our personalities, perspectives, goals, objectives

Hopes and dreams align like planets

Let my soul bounce off yours as

The sun skips on a river

Caresses her and graces his touch down deep

Let there be a mesmerizing eclipse

By the meeting of our lips

Let our joy be infinite as the times

You can encircle the path of a ring

Now that's a special thang.

Boy, what's in your soul?

I can see

What's in your soul is a reflection of me

-My King

Chapter Seven: The Replenishing

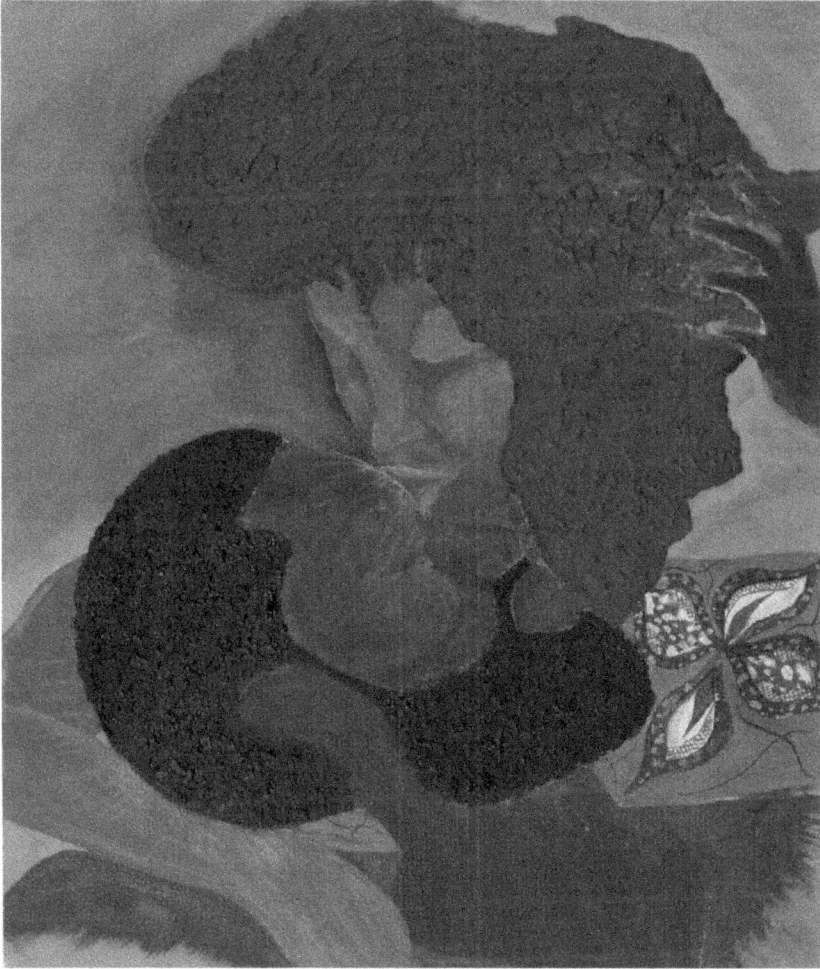

I'm that weirdo

Who gets turned on by a door

Opened as I stroll into a room

By a man who perceives more than

He reveals

Listens more than he speaks

Gives more than he receives

And removes my coat while

Placing his hand on my lower back

A man who hears words I have never spoken

A man who elicits emotions

I forgot were mine

Who observes every

minute detail of my being

As if he will earn a doctorate on me

I'm that weirdo who gets turned on

By a man

Strong and affectionate

He kisses my body and my spirit

And would fight to the death

To protect my honor

A man who

enjoys inspiring, witnessing, and savoring

The rays of my smile

The melody of my laughter

The songs of my soul

Who appreciates my style

Who shares more than I expect

Gives his advice when I need it

His wisdom, I receive it

His loving embrace, I crave it

I am that weirdo

who is turned on by a gentlemen

Who can carry his crown and his heart

Who conjugates his verbs

Who knows when to save,

and when to invest

And when to splurge his affection

Attention, devotion on me

Who heals me with his presence

A man who can trace my body

With his tongue

And pull down my panties with his teeth

All while caressing my soul

I am that weirdo who gets turned on

By a man whose actions answer my questions

Before I ever need to ask

Who cares for my heart, my mind, and my body

Who sees my needs as an extension of his

Whose love is deep, pure, flowing freely

Washes me from my past

Propels me towards my future

Purifies my hope

I'm that weirdo who craves a King

Because I am a Queen

Chapter Seven: The Replenishing

Defining my purpose is not the same as acting on it

Spiritual Growth is not the same as Self-Development

All the spiritual consciousness

in the world

is nothing without action

Action is the prescription for success

and the antidote of despair

No one wants to live a life of ambiguity

Who wants to live a life of, "We will never know what

could have been."

So sadly often preceded by "I've always been this way."

What about your life unlived?

Who you could be?

Your gifts only make room for you, if you get out of the

way

Aren't you afraid to die and the world- or better yet Your

World- Your loved ones, your family, your acquaintances

Never know who you really are

And you never get to live in the bliss

Of doing what you were created to do

That special joy

Never getting to experience your passions, your
contributions

Your unique talents, innate gifts lovingly shared with the
world

Get comfortable with being uncomfortable

How is playing small suiting you?

Is it working out for you?

You know doing the same thing over and over and over
again

But expecting different results is the definition of
insanity, right?

If you are to truly be the person you always knew deep
Down inside you could be

You are going to have to go places you have not been

Meet people you have not met

Do the things you have not done

Say things you have yet to say

And finally believe what you have yet to believe

Break the chains, start with this one

You are enough right now

You are perfectly imperfect

And someone out there needs what you have right now

Chapter Seven: The Replenishing

You are completely loved and loveable

Let's apply the faith that you celebrate in others

You are a love letter from God personified

And the time for your FAITH walk is now

Don't limit God

Don't limit yourself

God-given genius is not the same as

Doing it

Knowing is your comfort blanket while you watch the

storm outside

However, Doing is wrapping yourself in your dream and

going out

to conquer the storm

       -I traded my comfort blanket for living in my

       dream

Creation Mode

When I know

That I must no longer

stand guard

All throughout the

Day and

All throughout the night

to

Protect my vision

Prove my worth

Hide my flaws, mistakes, missteps

Defend my honor

I get to just create, give, share

Explore

Just wander

Just be me

Expand my heart

Unzip my chest and

Share my passions with the world

I give myself permission

To like me

To love me

Chapter Seven: The Replenishing

To take an idea all the way

Savor every morsel of life

Enjoy the Sun

And the twinkling stars at night

I give myself the privilege

The distinct honor of loving myself lavishly

Chapter Eight: The Eroding

Chapter Eight: The Eroding

It's a sad thing when you're perfect for someone

But their detrimental for you

You are their light

And they are your smoke

Chapter Eight: The Eroding

You flew in too swiftly

Your care was the other missing wing

And off we flew to heaven

Suddenly your heart changed

Love was gone

And I crashed straight to HELL

       -Burnt by an over-lit candle

Chapter Eight: The Eroding

I gave you the keys to my heart

I shared; you hoarded

You left and locked me out

To go visit other fires

Chapter Eight: The Eroding

The deepest cut

Is always the first one

A slash straight to my center

A samurai sword of precision

You wielded the blade like surgeon

And ninja

The heartbreak

Crushing Betrayal

of friendships which never evaporated naturally

Never blew away like petals

They were strategically

An ni hi lated

I had to blow dust away

after the explosion

With a few words

You dropped a bomb on

Our infant love

Raw, open, exposed

Destroyed

I Frankensteined myself

Back together

To give you friendship

But your tongue kept slicing

My flesh

Now gashes instead of scratches

I ran away in terror

A monster in search of love

Healing

Because soon I'll be no more than

Another martyred heart

Staked and burned

Sacrificed to the flames

By another soul

　　　　　-Hurt

Chapter Eight: The Eroding

He wanted to live

In my heart

But he couldn't enter

Holding all that rage

Chapter Eight: The Eroding

She is on trial

Even now

All around the world

All day and all night

she is on trial in your home

And on your job

for crimes she never committed

she has been locked up

Freed and then locked up again

Faster than we blink

she has a wrap sheet so long

She spends her nights in jail

For charges upon charges

With no defense

she stands there with tears in her eyes

With outstretched hands

As you hurl insults at her

as you tell her all the pain

All the suffering

You show her the scars and

You yell, "They hit me."

she listens; and mouths, "They hit me too."

They lied on me

she repeats, They lied on us.

They ignored me

she repeats, They ignored us

They shut me out

she whispers barely audible, they shut us out

They abused me

she cries, they abused us

she sobs forgive them

and reaches her arms out to hug you

Yet you slap her hands away

and spit in her face

You smile as the judge declares

Guilty

You dance as she is hauled away

She sobs bitterly

For she knows when you lock her up

You let hate run free

You lock away all your hope

You lock away all of your healing

Without her, you'll never forgive

You'll never be free

Chapter Eight: The Eroding

Your pain clouds your judgment

And without her you will live

in your own prison of anger and bitterness

And soon you will hurt someone else

A vicious cruel cycle

So please free my homie Love

She's innocent

and all her charges are Trump-ed.

in fact she was the victim too

She shared in all the pain

She wanted to help carry your burdens

She just desired to help heal your pain

She knows, hate wins when you lock her away

Her name is Love

And she's been writing letters to the whole world

Delivered between two thighs every second

Even in her captivity

Loves been suffering too long

Love keeps no record of your wrongs

Love is patiently waiting to be set free.

Love is the kindest one I know.

Chapter Eight: The Eroding

Love has counseled and healed so may but she doesn't
brag.
Love selflessly shares all she has with the other prisoners.
Love is meek and celebrates truth.
Love trusts, hopes, perseveres, and protects endlessly.
When can we fight to set love free?
The prosecution rests their case
The jury declares guilty
And the judge sentences love to Life without parole
But we couldn't allow this
We had to break love out because
She was, is, and always will be innocent
Hate, Hurt, Denial, Jealousy, and Envy did all those things
To create evil
because if Love is imprisoned
than compassion goes too
And humans become evil without compassion
So we, Faith and Hope
had to set Love free

-Love Has Been on Trial

110

Chapter Eight: The Eroding

The most turbulent waters

cannot quench Love

But your care fades quick

Chapter Eight: The Eroding

Mt. Calvary

Valley Rose

Gospel Water Branch Baptist

New Zion Hill

Greater Young Zion

The Christian City of Praise

Tabernacle Baptist

The Potter's House

Have I had enough church yet?

Can I live it now?

Outside the walls?

With all this church in my bones

Can I love my neighbor yet?

How many concordances can I read?

Before I learn how to love

The neighbor I walk over

Everyday as I sprint

To the church house

     -Over-churched yet Under-loved

You owe me

You owe me

You owe me

Cut my check

There's a love deficit

I Am love

Why would you dare

Come praise me

And not love your

Neighbor

You walk over them to

"Love" me?

You spit in my face

What profits

A man to gain the world and lose

his soul

What profits a woman to gain the world

And lose her soul

Without love you are nothing

All your prophecies

Fail

Your idol worship

Vain

Your riches

Expire

Your connections

Wither

Charity

Love begins at home

I know your heart

I see it

I made it

I know what it is capable of

And you dare not surrender

It to me?

Love covers all

It inspires all

Encourages all

It's a light in a dark land

And comfort in a storm

How dare you hold back

From loving each other

I commanded you to

Love one another

I put that over all others

A commandment I gave to you

Along with free will

Because I love you

I fashioned your heart to

Be delicate

Pure, intricate, sustaining

Renewing

And you would reject love

You are not just to love

But become it

They are suppose to know you

By your love

I placed your heart in the center

For all roads lead to love

You owe me

You got me messed up

Trying to be puffed up

My reputation is on the line

You owe me

Love honors restores renews

I poured out my love

For you to be your best

And you'd rather beat your chest

And you want to rule

You know not to kill

But you are killing spirits

Hopes And futures

Your lack of love

Destroys what you are suppose

To be building

You are only giving drops of love

When I gave you oceans

Love never fails

People are starving for a

pure love

They never had

And you were supposed

To be that love

Real love can identify with real love

And I don't even recognize you

I am Love

Love is the way

Love is the truth

Love is the light

You owe me

Love now

Love is time sensitive

Critical for your survival

Then your Thrival

Love like your life depends

On it

Because it does

Love will set your dreams free

Love will set your gifts free

Love is me

Love will set you free

You owe me

Chapter Eight: The Eroding

That fiery tongue

Can cut down empires

And destroy souls

It's lashes sting longer

Than the lashes we can see

It divides

What was once indivisible

That charming tongue

Can write rubber checks

Can enter doors immaturely

Can con even the wisest

Can give you what you want

All the while taking away what you need

That honest tongue

Can set captives free

Can cut bone from marrow

Can cut the good from the bad

The growing from the decaying

That lying tongue

Can soil the work of the good

Waste so much time

Promote mass deception

And create more hurt

The encouraging tongue

Speaks life into dead endings

Dead places

Dead people

Rejuvenates dreams

Ignites the spark of discovery

Renews passions

Unites hopes, families, destinies

Back together

That loving tongue

Speaks healing for

Shipwrecked souls

Speaks abundant life

Plants gardens in barren

Lands

Pushes compassion

Over judgment

Translates wisdom for

Whatever ear is listening

Promotes wholeness

For whole people

Chapter Eight: The Eroding

With all these languages

With all these words to choose from

Which tongue will you use?

Chapter Nine: The Restoration

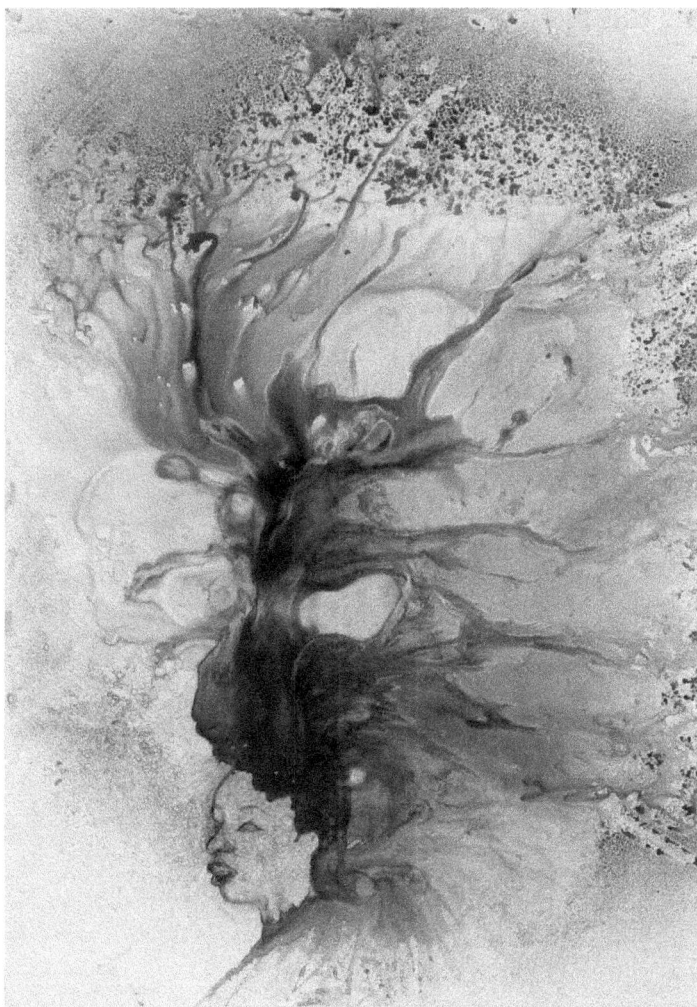

Chapter Nine: The Restoration

Lay your treasure by my well

Whisper the secrets you long to tell

Lean in and see yourself

Kiss my spirit

Chapter Nine: The Restoration

We enjoyed the fan's breeze

On this island of sheets

Touched ecstasy where our bodies meet

Safe and warm in these four corners

We form our own sovereign nation of two

Outside may be cold, but here I am warm

Wrapped around you

Here in our refuge, I am safe

To explore

To breathe deep where I hold my dreams

And my dreams hold me

Here we share the secrets you can only share

Skin to skin

- Island for Two

Chapter Nine: The Restoration

You may complement my completion

complement my completeness

For I am already whole

   I offer the advice to love me or leave me

I must shine both night and day

As stars do

I walk

where others dare not tread

I have been chosen

Buffed, and ground into refinement

I shine as royalty and a peasant's hope

For my grandeur is not in my garments

I dine with kings

and queens

I cherish a friend's dinner table

I live on love

I'll die for my convictions

I've soured mountains

and spent sleepless nights in the valleys

I know both the pain of defeat

And the heavy glory of success

I've selected the target and

Chapter Nine: The Restoration

I've missed the goal

time and time again

Yet I set the arrow on the bow again

And shot again for the stars

I get tired and may want to quit

But I don't know how

I don't breathe failure

I invest in quality

Not quantity

My home is my refuge

I rest to renew my mind and my body

I invest in myself

I seek out and carefully select my education

I eat the meat and leave the bones

Discernment

I continuously study and master my craft

A lifelong learner

There is no limit on my learning and what I can do

I stay ready for the next task

I watch, fight, and pray

I stay prepared

For opportunity

Chapter Nine: The Restoration

She need not knock

Because I tackle her outside

I trust my creator has made me for this time

My affirmations may seem a rant

Yet they are my mantra

A stream of consciousness of my dreams

And visions

I wear as pearls on my neck

That form my purpose

I am dualistic

Both of ambition

And servitude

I have found comfort living

On the eye of a needle

I believe anything is possible

I see opportunity when others merely

See a possibility

I feel overwhelming love

I've embraced my childlike wonder and curiosity

I take flying leaps into the unknown

I contribute to something bigger than myself

I create. I learn. I grow. I do.

Chapter Nine: The Restoration

I constantly evolve.

I believe it's never too late to start living the dream!

I create me

I AM

I AM

I AM.

-A Woman of Distinction

ABOUT THE AUTHOR

Tishun Nikco

Tishun Nikco is a Texas transplant and a Georgia native who happily blooms where she is planted. This young woman is an innovator who illuminates any room she enters. She is a self-taught writer and artist whose work comes straight from her soul. Tishun Nikco is also an avid gardener and her plants are luscious and vibrant. Her intention is for her work to nourish our souls and inspire us to add more love into our daily lives.

Tishun Nikco is a spiritual teacher and speaker of From Your Core Coaching and Consulting. She facilitates courses on living wholly from your core, healing, and uncovering your purpose. In addition, Tishun Nikco embodies healing through art. She leads creative workshops as the founder of A Lil' More Paint, a mobile all-encompassing art studio.

With a lil' more paint and a lil' more time, the picture comes into focus. She joyfully guides the participants through how to create their own works of contemporary art.

Tishun Nikco hopes to ignite a healing revolution. She believes that we should all lead in love.

Enjoy more of Tishun Nikco's artwork, poetry, and speaking on tishunnikco.com.

ABOUT THE ARTWORK

The Artwork featured for the Chapter
Openings in this book *There is Life in This
Water* is from the signature art series There is
Life in This Water. Chapters are listed below
with corresponding **artwork titles.** Artwork
is multi-medium in fluid watercolors.

ABOUT THE TYPE

This book was set in Garamond, a typeface designed by Claude Garamond in the 16th Century. Garamond designs had special characteristics like scooped and rounded serifs, slanted spaces inside the e and a particularly. Claude Garamond handcrafted metal punch cuts and matrices for his unique typefaces used in the printing of many books in Roman and Latin. Garamond is a modern typeface of many variations inspired by the calligraphist aesthetic and easier to use with printing presses.

www.ingramcontent.com/pod-product-compliance
Lightning Source LLC
Chambersburg PA
CBHW070045100426
42740CB00013B/2809